Name _____

1. Trace

2. 🖍️

3. ✂️

1

**Name** _____

1. Trace
2.
3. ✂

2

Name _____

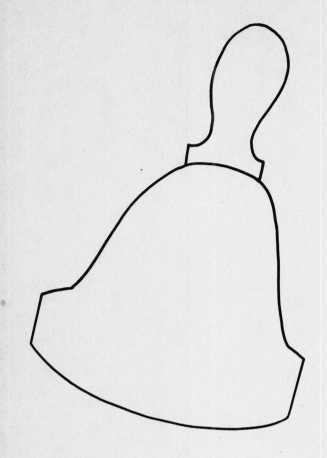

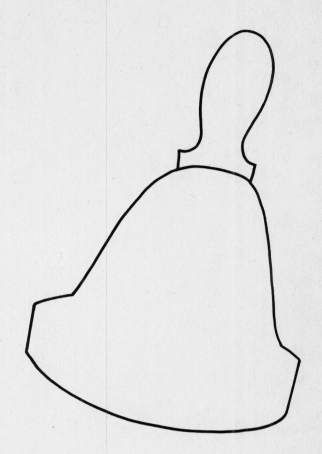

✂ - - - - - - - - - - - - - - - - - - - - - - - - - - - - - - - - - - - - - - - -

1.

2.

3.

3

Name _____

1.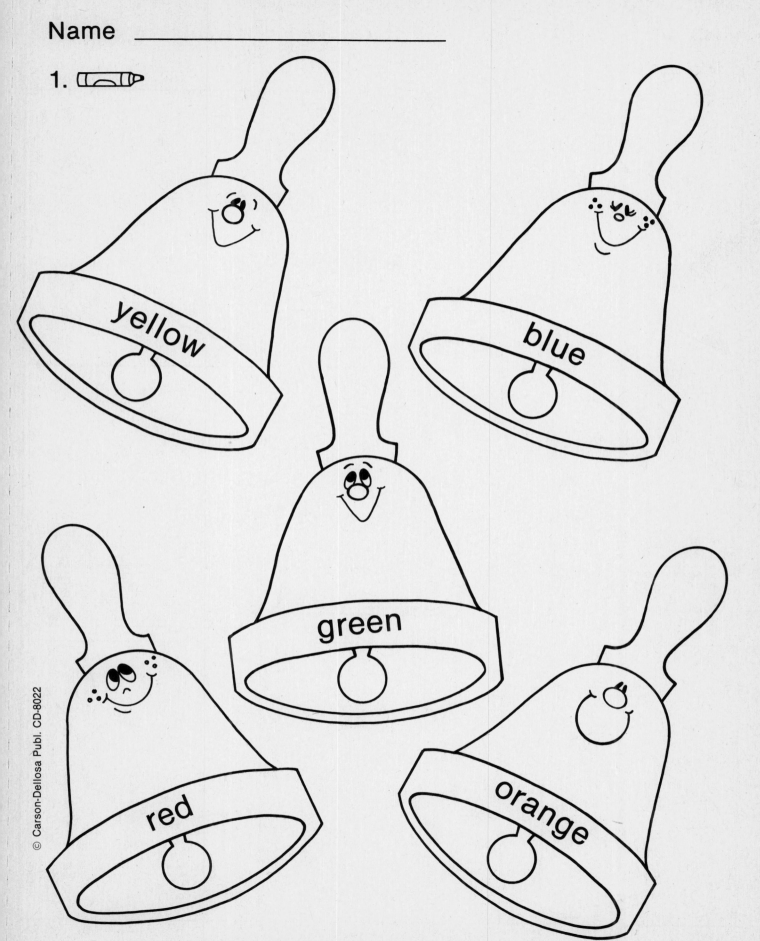

Name _____

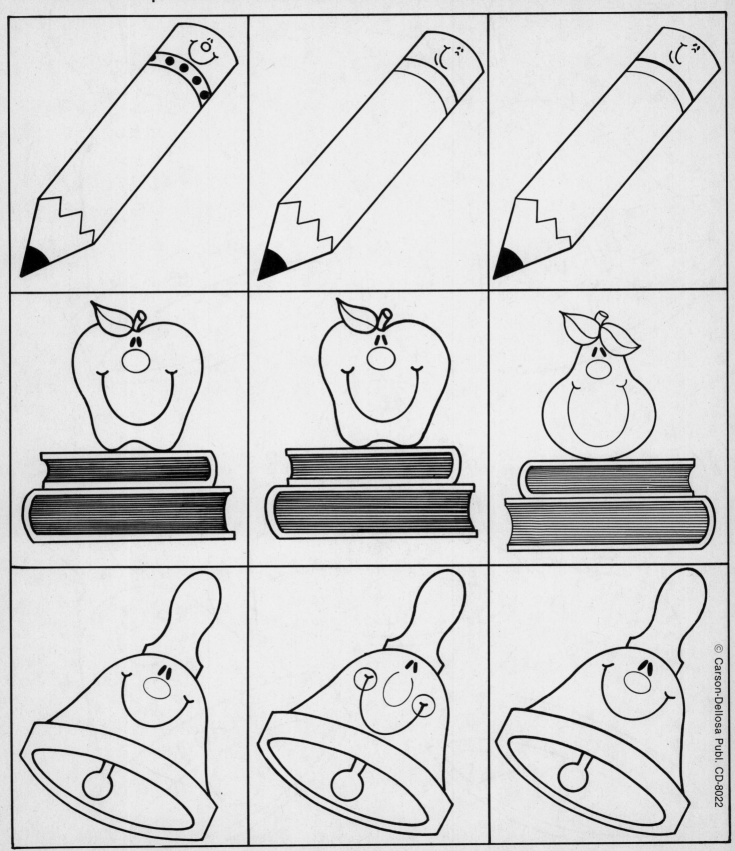 the pictures in each row that look the same.

5

Name _____

1. Trace
2.
3. ✂

6

Name _____

1. Trace

2.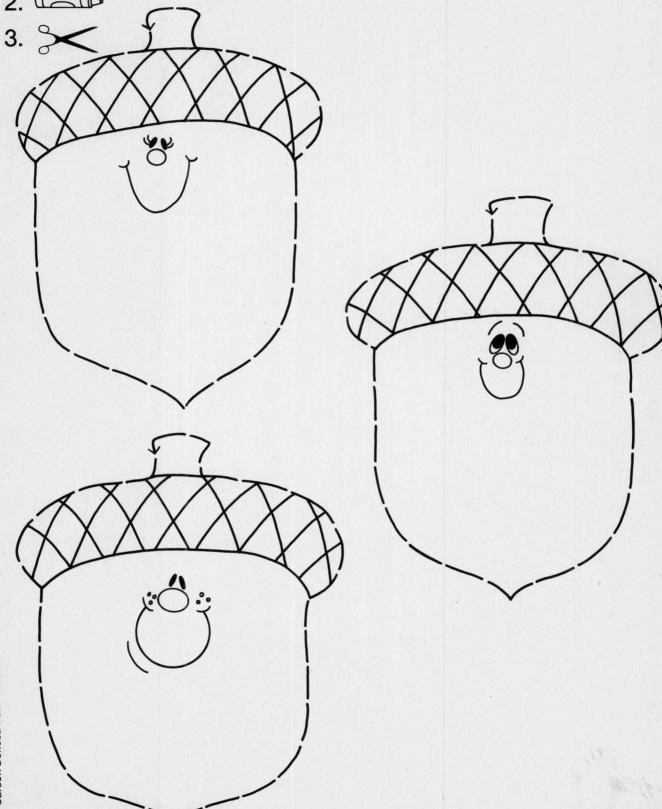

3. ✂

7

Name _____

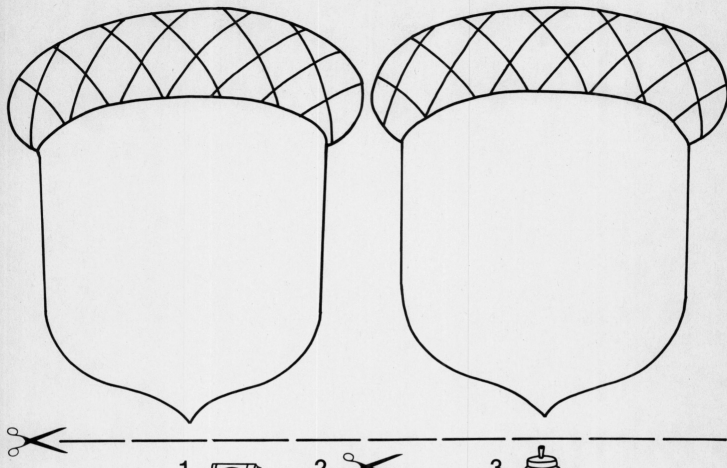

1.    2.   3.

**Name** _____

1.

brown      orange

yellow

red      blue

Name _____

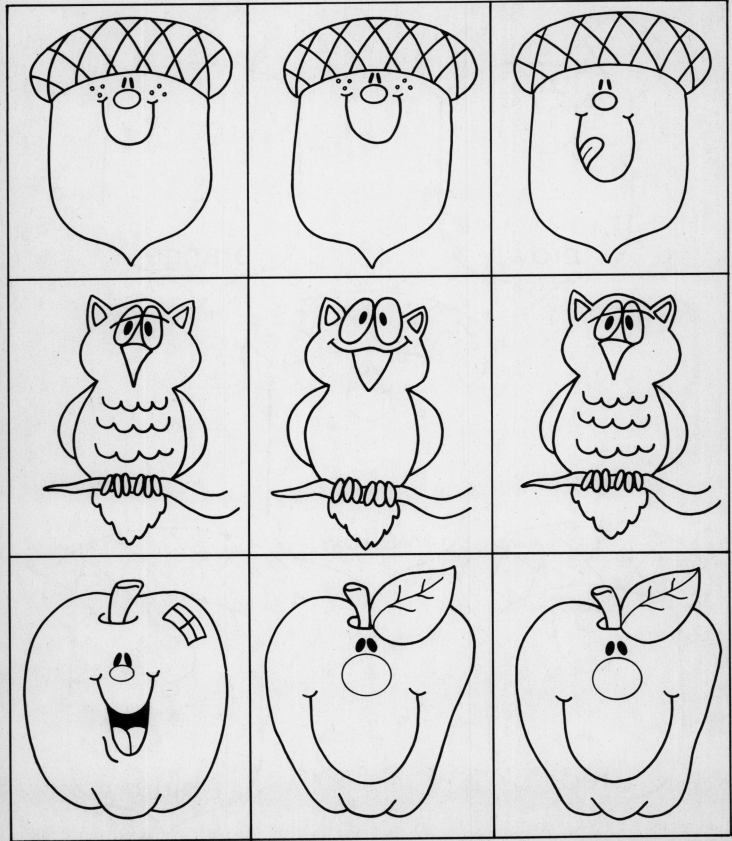

🖍 the pictures in each row that look the same.

1. Trace
2.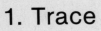
3.

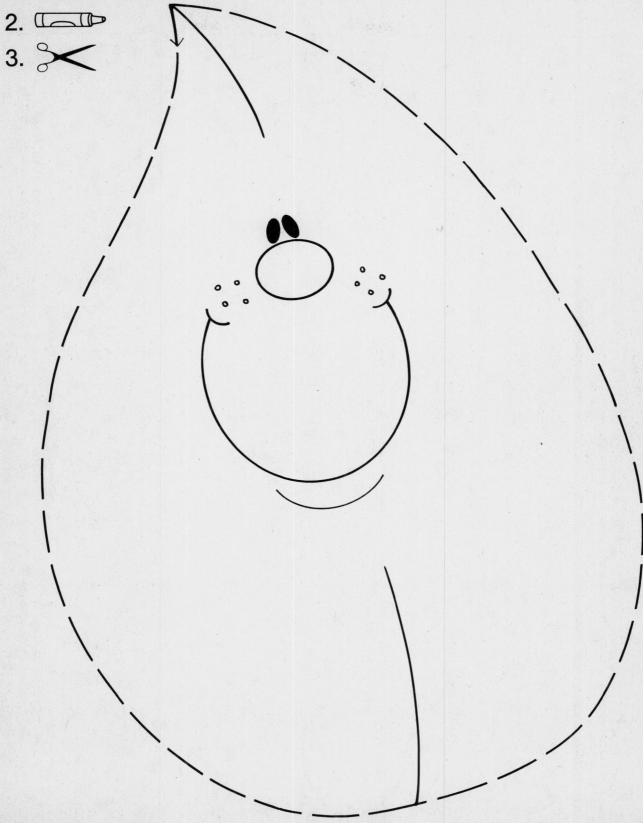

Name _____

1. Trace

2.

3.

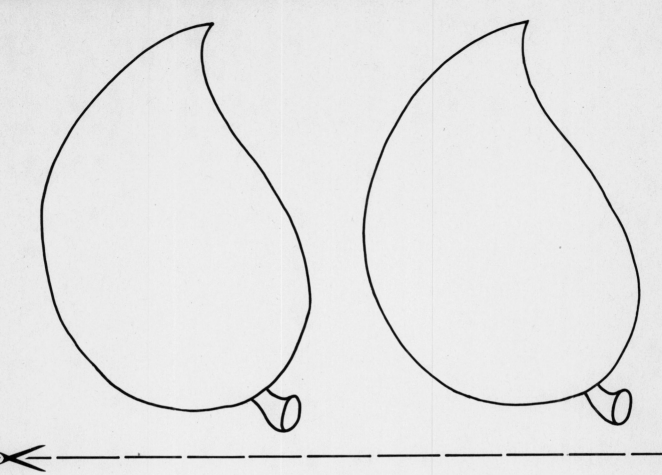

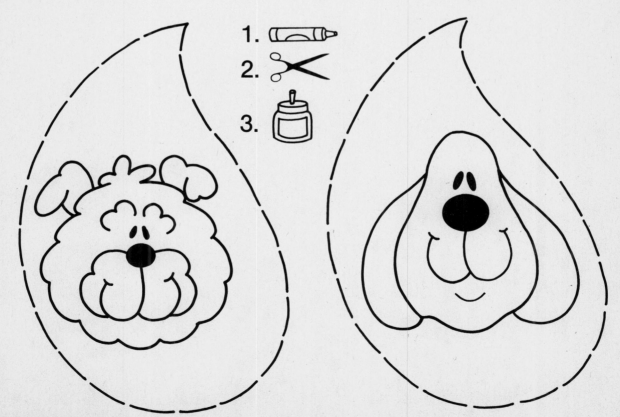

1. 
2. 
3.

1.

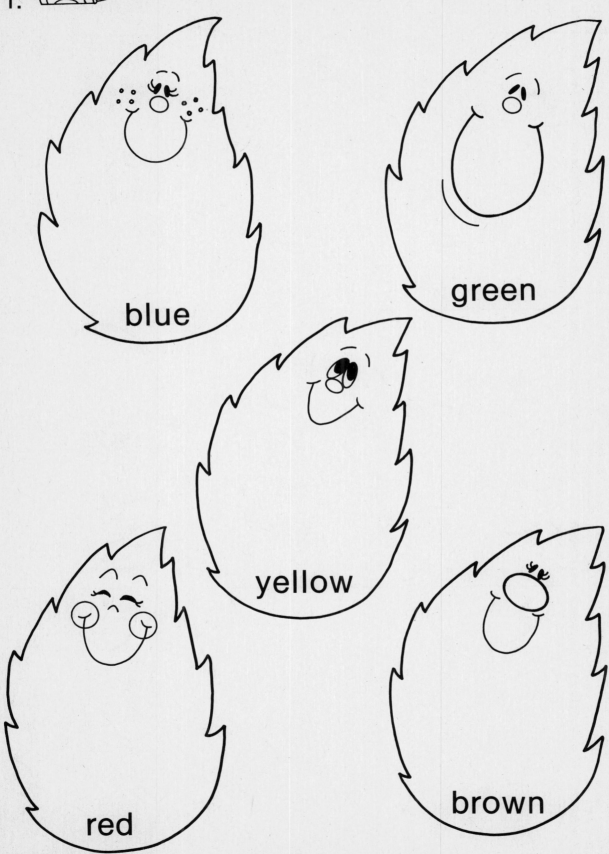

blue

green

yellow

red

brown

🖍 the pictures in each row that look the same.

# Name _____

1. Trace
2. Draw lines to connect the pictures that look the same.
3.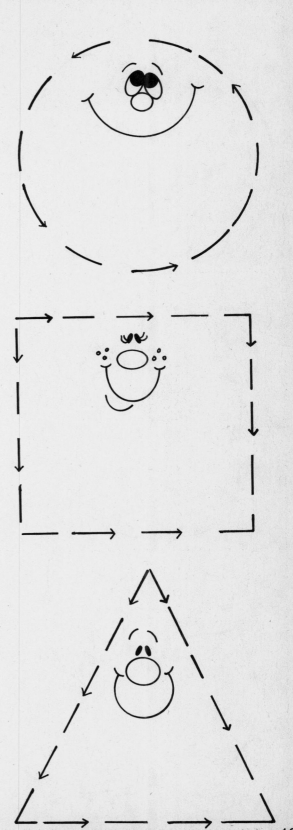

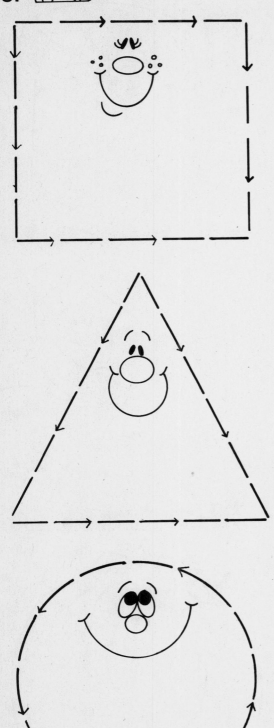

Name _____

1. Draw lines to connect the pictures that look the same.
2.

Name _____

1. Count the △s. There are _____ △s.

2.  the △s blue.

3. the rest of the picture any colors except blue.

Name _____

1. Count the ☐s. There are _____ ☐s.
2.  the ☐s red.
3. the rest of the picture any colors except red.

19                                    © Carson-Dellosa Publ. CD-8022

Name _____

1. Count the ◯ s. There are _____ ◯ s.

2. ▱ the ◯ s yellow.

3. ▱ the rest of the picture any colors except yellow.

Name _____

1. Count the pictures. There are ___ pictures.

2. ✏️

Name _____

1. Count the pictures. There are _____ pictures.

2.

Name _____

1. Count the pictures. There are _____ pictures.
2.